cjanasdreams.p

MW01230996

http://cjanasdreams.wordpress.com

Me and My Dogs (Color)
ISBN-13: 978-1494286019
      10: 1494286017

Printed in the United States of America

Autobiography of Author

Janice Nadine Richards was born on August 17, 1950, in Butte, Montana, Silver Bow County. She was born to Fred Wilson Richards and Eleanor Edna Pritchert Richards. Her father worked at McKey printing and then for the Montana Standard Newspaper. Her mother was a homemaker and a professional seamstress. She has one sister, Jeanine Arlee Richards Schmidt, who is four years older, currently living in Missoula, Montana. She lived in her parent's home, on 604 Caledonia, Butte, Montana until she graduated from High School in 1968. She then left for College, where she attended Rocky Mountain College for two years studying music education, and then attended two years at Eastern Montana College to complete her special education endorsement, and reading endorsement. Both colleges were in Billings, Montana. She married her high school sweetheart, whom she divorced after fifteen years of marriage. She had two sons by him, Shawn Paul Koski and Michael Glen Koski. They are her only children and the love of her life. Janice became a special education teacher and taught until she retired in May of 2009. She has been very active with the Hispanic community, and taught English as a Second Language, for the College of Southern Idaho. She likes to travel, and has been to Mexico three times. She continues to learn about different cultures, and continues to share her life's experiences through her writing. She taught in Montana, Idaho, and Nevada, and currently resides in Rupert, Idaho. She visits Montana when ever possible. She has many hobbies; her first love is the piano.

Her second love has become her computer. There she spends time reminiscing about her childhood, and remembering life in the Rockies. She has also spent time writing, poetry, song lyrics, children's stories and finger plays, as well as novel manuscripts. She loves writing and will continue to write as long as her health and memory will allow her to do so. She likes learning and experiencing new things in life. She looks forward to working with different communities and traveling for book signings, guest lectures, and whatever new experiences may come her way. Her plans for the future include more poetry books, a sequel memoir of her young adult life, several children stories, and several books on education. She also contracts for free lance-writing assignments such as anniversary, wedding, memorial, and poems by request.

She can be found on twitter under authorconsult, on her own Blog site at **http://cjanasdreams.wordpress.com.** or on Facebook, chatting with family, friends other authors, artists and her readers. Her biggest challenge is new technology and aging gracefully. She wishes to thank everyone who has purchased her books

She appreciates everyone for their wonderful support.

Dedications

I would like to dedicate this book to all dog lovers.

I especially wish to dedicate this book to **my mother and father** who taught me that every life was important and should be treated with respect. I would like to dedicate it to my sister, who shared a passion for animals. I also dedicate this book to my son's **Shawn Koski** and **Michael Koski** who share a love for animals and have had a love for dogs.

I especially dedicate this book to all the people who save animals, work with the Humane Society and animals shelters so that animals can not only live with respect but also die with dignity; to the Veterinarians who make it possible for many animals to be saved. I thank all the volunteers who foster animals and help them find love and new families; the teachers who take time to teach about animals in their classes. Thanks to all people taking time to understand dogs and their behaviors; those caring enough to see that their dogs are given the proper health care, having them spayed, and neutered and teach their children to love animals. I dedicate this book to the dogs in my life that have made a difference to me.

I would like to give my thanks to **Tammie Strong** who assisted with the editing of this book.

A special thanks to my dad, **Fred Richards** who drew the pastel picture of my dog Lady that is on the front cover. His strong love and compassion for animals will always be a part of me. Thank you dad, for being who you were, and showing me the way. I will never forget the values you taught me.

Watch for the up coming books:

*Poetry
"The Land of Horses"
"Grandma's Pantry"
"A Tribute to Those Serving the Red, White, and Blue"

*Memoirs
"Growing Up in the Rockies"
"Coming of Age in the Rockies" The Rebel Years
"Try Walking in my Shoes"

*Children's Stories
"Mercedes"
"Children's Books" (Yet to be disclosed)

Educational & Life Experiences
"Fun Things to Learn"
"Secrets behind Close Doors"

"Short Stories"
"The Cat in the Box"
"Me and My Dogs"

Table of Contents

"Me and My Dogs"

By

Janice N. Richards

Mechanically Autographed

Best Wishes From

Janice N. Richards

Overview

This book was written out of my love for dogs. It will tell you how I was raised around dogs. I will share with you why I truly believe that dogs are important in our lives. Through out the book I will talk about dogs I have owned and dogs that I have known. I will share with you a dog's routine, the most common dog behaviours and suggestions for feeding your canines. In no way do I claim to be an expert on animals and this information has either been from living with animals or reading about them. I hope that this book will help the reader to learn that all animals have feelings, needs, and should be treated with dignity. Most of all I hope to help the reader understand the differences in dogs from other animals and to realize how smart they really are. My book has grown out of a love for dogs, and I hope that everyone can share that moment with me. The one thing that I have learned is that dogs are loyal to you. God Bless all you dog lovers out there and may you pass your love and understanding of dogs on to others. I hope you will learn to enjoy dogs as much as I do and laugh at their amusing antics. There is never a dull moment if you have dogs around. Their loyalty is why they are called "Man's Best Friend." Nothing is more comforting than to be greeted at the end of a long working day by one who is happy to see you and asks very little of you in return, only wanting a gentle pat on the head, a hello, some food, water and a place to call home with shelter through the storms. Dog's make the world a better place. They put a smile on your face when you've had a rough day. They make you feel loved no matter what. Thanks to all the dogs who are loyal friends.

Chapter 1 "Growing Up Around Dogs"

*When I was growing up, we always had a dog in our home. My father had been raised around dogs and he shared his love of dogs with me. My father had a natural ability for training a dog and earning their loyalty and respect. One whistle was all it took and the dog would be at his feet. After all, he had a distinct whistle that was natural. He would place his fingers in his mouth and let out the loudest whistle you'd ever heard. Everyone in the neighbourhood recognized it. Later on, he would teach me how to whistle that way. He had grown up with dogs of all sizes, shapes, and breeds. He loved to have dogs around the house. However, he believed in training them to obey and be well-behaved animals. Some people might have called him a "Dog Whisperer" as they all responded to his wants and needs. However, my mother didn't like animals in the house, so they came to a mutual agreement. If the weather was nice, the dog was outside. If the weather was bad, the dog either went into the basement or came into the kitchen but could not enter the carpeted area of the house. Mother didn't believe in having animals on the furniture or in the beds. That was a definite "**No**," even when company came to stay with us. We lived in the Rocky Mountains where it was very cold and winters were long. The dogs would need to be in the house for protection from the elements. Where we lived, everyone had a dog and at that time, there were no leash laws. It was common to see a dog in every yard or out running in the streets. Wherever the kids were playing, you would find the dogs too. We learned early how to handle dogfights, and to get out of the way. We learned to grab the water hose and spray the dogs* to break up the fights. Dogs were just a normal way of life back in those days. Most of the dogs were "Heinz 57," which meant they were a mixture of breeds and you probably didn't know for sure what they were. What was important was that you trained your dog correctly and didn't teach your dog to go after cats. The boys in the neighbourhood liked to tell the dogs to "sic the cats," and soon, the dogs would go chasing some poor cat up a tree. That was considered bad behaviour and not acceptable for dogs. Dogs for the most part ran freely and not too much was thought about it as long as they didn't bite anyone. However, the smaller dogs were usually kept at home even though they had a big bark to them. They didn't realize they were small and needed some protection. Mainly you would see Collies, Shepherd mixes, Boxers, a few Bulldogs, and Labradors. I only had two bad dog experiences growing up. One was when I would walk to elementary school, there was a Labrador dog that loved to come running out and jump on your back as if it was going to hump you. That terrified me. The other incident was when I was a little older and played on the playground behind our house. One day before dinnertime a Black Labrador came running from nowhere and was angry and foaming at the mouth. All of the kids ran to the top of the slide. I was the first on the slide so I had to hang on for dear life as not to be pushed off. My mother came to the fence and called me to come home. About that time, the police arrived with the dogcatcher. It was one of the neighbour's dogs that had gotten out. She had always been a good dog and had many litters. They said that after her last litter was taken away she went mad. I don't know if that is the truth or not but she was put to sleep. I would grow up not liking

Labradors although I would have more than one encounter in my lifetime with them with different family members. I was thankful that I had been raised around dogs and had a love for them before those incidents. Having been taught that a dog was a family member I never thought any different until I grew up, moved away from home, and realized not all communities were the same. I loved dogs, they loved me, and that was really all that mattered. I saw dogs as a normal part of our family life and everyone had their own role and spot in the family. We always taught the dogs to travel with us in the car and that made it easier when my dad wanted to go on vacations. The dogs always liked to go for a good ride and hated to be left at home alone, after all family is family and all wanted to be part of the daily activities.

Chapter 2 "Frisky"

When I was born, my family already had a dog-named Frisky. Frisky had come to our home unexpectedly. A family was moving and couldn't take Frisky with them. They didn't want to take him to the animal shelter. My Aunt Mamie knew the family. Well, dear Auntie Mamie brought the dog to my dad. "Frisky" was going to be a gift for my sister who was about three at the time. This didn't make my mother happy. However, my father took the dog and Frisky became part of our family. I grew up with him and loved having him around. My father said, "Frisky" was a "Heinz 57", however, as I look back now I think he was part Collie and part Australian Shepard. "Frisky" didn't seem to me as big as a full-grown Collie but was bigger than a Border Collie; however, I was young and am relying on my memory after many years. He was as black as the Ace of Spades with a little white on his stomach, if I remember correctly. He had a bushy tail that could knock you over in a moment. He loved to run with the kids out in front of the house. However, "Frisky" had two bad habits. He liked to chase cars, and he liked to fight other dogs. If another dog came down the street, he'd push us kids out of the way with that tail and jump in between so we couldn't get hurt. Soon everyone would be running for hoses or buckets of water to break up the dogfights. He never chased cats until the boys in the neighbourhood started "sicing" him on them. Then that became his third problem. The neighbours had a dog-named "Butch". "Frisky" hated that dog. The two dogs loved to fight.

The only thing between the two dogs was an old wood fence that was about to topple over at any minute. It wasn't hard for the two dogs to get at each other. The fence was actually the neighbour's fence. She was a widow and had five children to support, so my dad didn't want to worry her about the fence. He spoke to the neighbour and asked if it would be all right to put up a chain link fence thinking that would keep "Frisky" in our yard and the two dogs apart. It was agreed on, my father went to work pouring cement, and putting in the posts then putting the chain link fence up in its place. All appeared to be well. However, now both dogs could look at each other through the fence. It was a six-foot chain link fence and my father thought it was high enough on the cement base to keep both dogs in their own yard. Well, "Frisky" proved him wrong when he sailed over the fence to get into the neighbours yard and fight their dog "Butch". Now there was no way of keeping "Frisky" in the yard when he wanted out although several times he didn't clear the fence and got caught on the top of it, but he always managed to get himself off. Then he would run loose in the neighbourhood. However, if my father was home all it took was one good whistle and "Frisky" would come running. He respected my father and knew he'd better come when called. "Frisky" was scared of one thing that I remember and that was thunder. He would always get into the house and hide behind the old bathtub with the claw feet or the stove in the kitchen. It took hours to get him out of there. One time, just as it began to thunder the neighbour opened her door and he ran into the neighbour's house. We couldn't get him out until much later when my dad came.

The neighbours had to lock their dog, "Butch," on the back porch, to keep the two dogs apart. My dad liked to use treats with his dogs and he would hide them to see if they could find them in his pocket or behind his back, etc. "Frisky's" favourite treat was graham crackers. My mother had a bottom cupboard where she kept the crackers and it was just before you entered the front room. Now "Frisky" was not allowed past the kitchen so he would lie in front of the cupboard and put his head into the dining room area where he could watch everyone. As long as he did not enter the carpeted area, my father would reward him with a graham cracker before bedtime and that would be that. My father always made dog beds from cardboard boxes. He put old blankets in them, and set them in the corner of the kitchen so the dogs knew their place. "Frisky" would get his can of dog food when we ate supper along with some dry food, which was left down all day. Then he would spend his day out in the yard when the weather was nice. Sometimes my father would put him in the basement. I remember one time when he didn't come home for several days and my father went looking for him. "Frisky" had been in a very bad dogfight and dad kept him down in the basement until he was healed. Dad didn't want us kids to see "Frisky", nor did he want him to get out and fight again. It was a bad situation and I could tell that dad was worried about him. However, you couldn't break "Frisky" from fighting after all he was a strong Alpha Dog and he had learned to prove his right to his territory. All you could do was to try to keep him safe. Then as "Frisky" became older, his legs started to be crippled and he could no longer run and enjoy the life he had known.

My father looked at my mother and said it's time to put him down. My father didn't believe in letting an animal suffer. It was hard on the entire family but I think it was harder on my father than anyone else since they had become so close. "Frisky" was my sister's dog and she loved him. I was the tag along I loved having him around. None of us wanted to see him in pain. When "Frisky" was put to sleep, it was the end of an era for the neighbourhood because he had always made it know he was the Alpha Dog. The neighbourhood was his territory. Some didn't miss him, but all remembered him and how he use to roam freely. The one thing that I will remember most is that my father taught us how to love animals and he set the example with "Frisky". That would affect my entire life and my love for animals that would follow.

"Frisky", "We love you and may you run freely in Dog heaven!"

Chapter 3 "Heidi"

Now that "Frisky" was gone, my sister wanted another dog. She was in junior high. I was in the elementary school. My mother said, "Why should we get another dog?" "I will be the one who ends up taking care of it. " Well someone had heard about a litter of Cocker Spaniels that were free. I went with my sister and dad to look at them. They were so cute. This, of course, started an argument, as I wanted my own dog and so did my sister. We were told we had to share. That meant my sister got the choice of the litter. However, I always loved the runt, which "Heidi" turned out to be. However, my sister would always refer to "Heidi" as her dog. I am not sure why but my mother decided to let "Heidi" be a housedog, but she could not be on the furniture. "Heidi" was a funny little puppy with brown and white spots, and big floppy ears. The first thing she did was to go into our bedroom and hide in the corner by the old heat duct that ran next to the wall. We had to climb on my bed to get her out. That's how she got her name since she was always finding a place to hide. My dad made a dog box that fit her, he put it in the kitchen and there she would sleep at night. However, she liked to be wherever the family was; she wasn't much of an outside dog. She liked being in the house. Her mother was a small cocker cross but we did not know what breed her father was, although, he must have been a larger dog. "Heidi" use to get so excited when we came home she would go racing through the house and slide on the linoleum floor. One day she hurt herself.

When all, her yelping stopped my parents took her to the Vet and he said her joints didn't fit her size. He said we would always have to be careful with her hind legs, as they would pop out of place. Therefore, we had to teach her not to race through the house. Once she stopped doing that, she was okay. "Heidi" was a very well- behaved dog. We played fetch with her and hid snacks for her to find and had a good time with her. However, she did have one very bad habit. She loved popcorn. Every year when Halloween rolled around my mother made her famous popcorn balls for the neighbourhood kids. If you were holding a popcorn ball in your hand, "Heidi" would snatch it out of your hand and eat it. That was the only time she ever got into trouble. However, we all thought it was funny because she only snatched mother's popcorn balls. "Heidi" was a loving dog. All she wanted was to be loved in return. She loved to sit and watch television with the family. She knew when it was bedtime to go to bed. My father had trained her well. The only time she barked was if someone came to the house or if she wanted outside. She knew her place and it made my mother happy. "Heidi" had a talent for being the "Ham" of the family. That would show when she refused to allow my sister's first boyfriend into the house. It was the first person we had ever seen her dislike and he would have to come with a bag of dog bones every time he came to the house or she wouldn't let him enter. She was a good judge of character as he turned out to be someone who would break my sister's heart in the end. They say animals are a better judge of people than humans are and I do believe that. We must have gotten "Heidi" when I was about twelve years old.

Eventually my sister would get married and move away leaving "Heidi" at home where I would have her all to myself. When I graduated from high school, she was still with my parents. Then one day I was talking to my mom from college and she told me "Heidi" had gotten sick. They had taken her to the Vet's; it was time to put her to sleep. The hardest thing for me was not being able to say goodbye. I loved that crazy little dog and I always will.

"Heidi" may you be happy in dog heaven and enjoy each day.

It's Dress up Time.

Janice puts a shirt on "Heidi."
"Heidi" would let you do just about anything.

"Heidi" playing with dad.
They loved their time together.

"Heidi" in the middle, with mom and Aunt Audrey.

"Heidi" with Janice at Christmas !

Curious "Heidi", wondering what's going on!

Dress up for the girls.
"Heidi" with Janice and Jeanine.

I Had a Little Dog

I had a little dog, her name was Heidi.
I loved her so, but she wasn't tidy.
She liked to play with toys everyday,
She liked to run, whenever she may.
She liked to hide in my bedroom,
The only way to get her was with a broom.
She always looked like she was laughing,
We didn't know if she was just panting.

She knew not to beg for table scraps.
She didn't dare jump into our laps.
Heidi had one weakness and we all new.
She couldn't resist a popcorn ball to chew.
Heidi couldn't wait for popcorn to fall.
She'd reach right up no matter how tall.
The next we knew she began to chew.
We all looked around to see what was new.

We all knew it was a popcorn ball gone,
There was nothing left to be done.
Everybody loved Heidi so,
No one could get mad and make her go.
So every year at Halloween,
My mother wouldn't scream.
That was the only time of year,
That Heidi knew her treat was near.

Heidi was a special friend,
Right up until the very end.

Chapter 4 "Flossy"

"Flossy" was my Aunt Mamie's dog. They lived with my grandmother. "Flossy," was another "Heinz 57" mix. My aunt rescued "Flossy's" mother from an abusive situation and there were four puppies. The mother was a Cocker and the puppies were crossed with a Boston Terrier. There were two long- hair puppies and two short- hair that resembled the Terrier mix. My father's family was always rescuing dogs. The family believed in caring for animals and treating them like family. My aunt also found a home for the mother. Homes were found for two of the puppies. My Auntie Mamie kept "Flossy," which was a long hair Cocker dominant dog that was black and white. She had big, floppy black ears, but she was mostly white. My Aunt Audrey ended up with one of the shorthaired Terrier mixes. Which they called "Slate" and I don't remember much about that dog. "Flossy" reminded me of "Heidi." She was fun to play with, and every time we went to visit my grandmother, "Flossy" would want to play. "Flossy" was a good dog and good company for my aunt and grandmother. For the most part, she had been raised right without any bad habits. However, she did have one special treat that she liked. She favored her ice cream cones. If my Auntie Mamie took a ride to the A & W, she always took "Flossy" with her. She would buy her a child's vanilla cone and the two of them would sit in the car eating their ice cream. If grandma had ice cream at home, it was hard to take it out and have a treat because "Flossy" would expect her ice cream too. It became the family joke. "Flossy" also liked to eat lettuce with dressing, and she

liked radishes too. She would go out into the yard when we would mow and plant flowers for my grandmother. She liked being around people. She would follow you in and out of the house no matter how many trips you made. She was known to be a good mouser. She liked being around people." Flossy" was part of the family for many years. After about twelve years, she got too old and sick. She was put to sleep, which was a sad day for everyone. She was Auntie Mamie's last dog. The house was never quite the same after "Flossy" was gone. However, she remained in our hearts and memories forever. Whenever I see a cocker with big black, floppy ears, I think of her and wonder if that dog likes ice cream cones too.

I hope they have ice cream cones in Dog Heaven for "Flossy"

Chapter 5 "Lady"

Now I was married and we finally had graduated from college. I was ready to start having my own family. We were in our first year of teaching. My husband and I went to the teacher's conference in October, which was held in Billings, Montana. I decided I wasn't going home without a dog. My husband didn't quite understand my demands, but he was gone most nights supervising band activities and traveling on buses chaperoning their activities. I was alone at home in a new town along the high lines. We lived twenty miles from the Canadian Border and twenty miles from North Dakota. I wanted a companion. My husband wasn't happy however; he agreed since he liked dogs. I called the local animal shelter and told them I wanted a small collie and asked if they had one explaining we would be leaving the next day. They said they had one and would have to get a hold of the foster family and call me back. Impatiently, I waited for the call to come. It didn't take long and they arranged to bring the dog to the motel. The minute the dog walked through the door I knew she was the one for me. She was a Border Collie Mix and approximately three months old. She had already been with three families and was extremely nervous. I loved her and my husband agreed she was a beautiful dog and at that moment, we agreed to give her a home, which we would never regret. She was such a beauty with her black, brown and white colors. Her stomach and legs were white. Her back was black but her face was mostly brown and the top of her head black. She spent the night in the motel with us and the next morning we headed for home. However, that *would be a trip we would never forget. I was use to traveling with my dogs and thought it was perfectly normal. However, this dog was so nervous that every time you reached for the dashboard or turned a knob she threw up. Thankfully, we had stopped and bought her a towel before leaving town. We would have to make many stops before arriving at home. Once home it was a relief to be there, needless to say, my husband was not happy. We pulled the car into the garage, which was attached to the house. We always went in the kitchen door. However, we had to pass the stairs to the basement, which this new family member would not do. It meant carrying her into the house every time we took her somewhere and carrying her to the car. She had a fear of stairs. This was when we decided someone had abused her. The Animal Shelter had given us no information on her, which would have helped us a lot. However, this beautiful dog always walked with her head held high so we named her "Lady" because she was one. She was already house broke and that was a relief so now it was simply a matter of getting her to work into our life style, playing with her, and teaching her to trust us along with some new tricks. For the most part everything went well. She wasn't allowed on the furniture and she knew it. She stayed inside while we were at work and I would hurry home to let her outside. We had a huge yard where she could run all she wanted too, however, on one occasion she was caught sleeping on our bed and that habit would be broken as she had an accident on our brand new mattress. On the weekends, my husband would take her to the dam and run her, which she loved.*

We had learned from the Vet that giving her a tranquilizer before traveling would avoid problems. One vacation break we were heading for home, which was a long trip, and we went to the Vet's to get the usual tranquilizer. The vet's assistant was filling in that day. He gave us a pill that was big enough for a horse. We were young and didn't know any better than to give it to her. She slept for twenty-four hours. I said she'd never take another tranquilizer after that and she didn't. She enjoyed the visits at grandma and grandpa's house but was always ready to go when the car left. We had a bedroom in our basement, which we had tried to leave her in during the day when we were at work, but she clawed the door until we had to fix the door so we figured it was better to leave her in the house around her familiar things. She had her bed and her toys. The end of the school year soon came and we moved back to our hometown area. She loved being around both families and children. She was happy if everyone was together. She would go around and count noses to see if everyone was there. It took us a full year to get her over the fear of stairs but she even overcame that. Then I became pregnant with our first child and I didn't work. She was happy as I was home everyday with her and I spoiled her. She was my dog from the start and always would be. When my son was born, we brought him straight from the hospital to my parent's home and "Lady" was there but he was asleep in the carrier so she didn't think anything of it as she really hadn't seen or heard him. Suddenly he started to cry, and she knew whatever was making such a fuss, was on the dining room table. She started racing around the table in circles.

I picked up the carrier and slowly lifted my new bundle of joy down for her to see where the noise was coming from, she gave the baby a big lick, and after that, they were best friends. When my second son was born, it was no longer new and she acted as if oh we have another one. "Lady" was so good. She let the boys lay on her, pull her hair, and grab her tail as she went running through the house. "Lady" never barked unless she heard a strange sound, then she would give a warning to everyone. It was wonderful having her as the boys grew up. I would always know where they were by where she was because she stayed close to them and in those days, there were no leash laws.

She loved being part of the family and that included riding in the car and going fishing. She had overcome her fear of riding and all you had to do was jingle the keys or say, "Do you want to go?" She would be at the door ready to go along before you could get there. She loved the freedom at the lake when we went fishing, but she had one bad habit. She would always find a dead fish to roll in, usually, just before we were getting ready to head for home. Then in the lake, she went for a bath. We always took her towel and some soap with us, and although she didn't like bathes, she never fought us over having one. She loved going to visit grandma and grandpa's house as much as she liked being at home. She had her own spot in the car and she knew where to lie down when visiting. She could even be taken to a motel and she knew how to behave. She was a joy to have around and she had completed my family. Then there was the day we had gone to the bread store in my parent's hometown and we bought a rack of bread not realizing how much bread there would be.

We were trying to save money and a rack was only $10.00 but it was a full backer's rack. It filled our entire Blazer; leaving little room for anyone. We stopped at my parent's home. We gave my parents bread, as we couldn't eat it all and we needed room for the kids in the car. During the hustle and bustle of everything, we forgot the dog. We had a thirty-mile drive home and half way there, we realized we were missing "Lady." We decided we were close enough to home to just go ahead and go home and unload the car put the kids to bed and my husband would go back for her. I felt horrible as if I had forgotten one of my children. I had tried to call my parents but got no answer. They had left right behind us. While we were unloading, the car they pulled up in front of our house with the dog laughing at us and asking if we forgot something. "Lady" was sure glad to be home with the kids. After that, I always counted noses. "Lady" didn't take to many men but she loved my dad and she loved my husband and the boys. Now when we moved to a larger town and the boys were a little older I depended on her to help me keep track of them. When the boys started to ride hot wheels down the sidewalk in front of the house, she would be running right behind them. She loved to go to the park with the family and her favorite activity was playing catch with the Frisbees. We couldn't have gotten a better dog no matter how we had planned it. However, I would always remember that she was my dog and that there would be times when I would have to protect her. I would always remember the time when I went out of town for a week to the Special Olympics for my job and my husband took care of the home and our first-born child.

It had upset her and she got diarrhea. The day I returned home no one was at the house and I was worried. I had also found out that morning that I was pregnant with our second child. Frantically I went running through the house and found a note from my husband, which said that he was out looking for "Lady" because she had run away. I came out the front door wondering which direction to walk as we only had one car. Just then, he drove past the house. I got in the car took my first-born son and said, "Let's go find her." He didn't know where to go. He said that he had yelled at her for having an accident in the house and put her outside in the yard. She had gotten out. I told him to drive down by our old house as the neighbor lady use to feed her bones. Just as we approached the old house there she was. She saw the car coming and was ready to run until I stepped out and called her to me. She came running and was so relieved to see me. We put her in the car and took her home. My husband made up with her that night. I realized then how much stability animals need. There would be another time when the boys got older that she had gotten out and went looking for them. They came home from school but there was no sign of her. We kept looking for her as it was the beginning of winter and the sun was going down. We knew the Montana nights were cold and we didn't want her left outside. We found here huddled up against the school. Once again she came when I called her and we took her home, loved her, and she was fine. She liked being surrounded by people and it was difficult when everyone was gone during the day. For a short period of time, we even had a kitten that loved to jump on her tail and ride through the house.

"Lady" didn't appreciate that kitten but she wouldn't harm it. She would just try to shake her tail and shake it off. "Lady" had learned to put up with just about anything that came her way. So many things took place while we had her. Now my husband worked nights after we moved to Billings and he was gone in the evening. I had hurried home one day after the day's activities and rushed into the house with the boys and forgot to lock the back door. It was my father's birthday and I wanted to call him before it got any later. The boys and I shared our birthday wishes and all was well. Then off to bed went the boys. They were about five and seven at this time. I was use to grading papers for school once the boys went to bed and I had all the lights on in the house. My husband got off work at midnight and it was nearing that time. All of a sudden, I heard "Lady" start to growl. I couldn't figure out what was going on, she never growled. I thought that maybe she heard my husband coming and yet that growling sound concerned me. She continued and her growl became louder and more aggressive and she started running back and forth between the kitchen and front room. I decided to get up and see what was going on and as I walked to the kitchen, I could see a man walking down my driveway, which led to the back door. I looked at the back door and it was wide open. I locked the door and called the police. She had stopped an intruder from entering the house. I was so thankful for having her at my side. My husband drove up to the house and saw the police, which worried him. When I explained what had happened he was relieved that "Lady" had done her job and protected everyone.

Then we went through a time with "Lady" when she was sick and we didn't know why. We took her to the Vet and he said she had tumors. We agreed to have them removed, as she was still a young dog. When he opened her up, he found out that she had a dozen fatty tumors the size of oranges. He removed them and closed her up. He cautioned us about them and said that she most likely would have more return. It was then that we agreed that quality of life was important and as long as she had quality of life, we would keep her alive. However, when the day came that she started to suffer we would ease her pain and have her put to sleep. "Lady" would be part of our family from October 1972 until June of 1986. My husband and I were going through a divorce. I had to leave for a job interview that was out of state, and I knew she couldn't make the trip. Her bladder and kidneys were starting to fail her. She was now 14 years old the best that we could figure. I gave my husband the choice of taking her until I got back or having her put down while the boys were gone and he had her put down which was for the best. There will never be another dog like "Lady" she was a perfect family dog and she knew how to show affection and her appreciation for being given a home. "Lady" lived up to her name and she always took care of my sons. She loved chasing balls and running behind the boys when they rode their bikes. I always knew where my kids were and that they were protected when we had "Lady" as she would never let anything happen to them. She had started out as our baby but had accepted each one of our boys when they were born. There wasn't a jealous bone in her body. She just wanted to be part of the family.

She listened and did what she was told to do. She loved to make everyone happy. She was as pure bred as they come. She knew how to walk, hold her head high and obey. She had a pride about herself.

"*Lady may you walk through heaven and enjoy each day because you earned it and you will forever be in my heart.*"

"*Shawn's first Christmas in Butte.*

There is nothing better than a dog protecting your child.

"Lady" getting her bath in Anaconda.
The kids are playing in the pool.

She may not like having a bath on a hot day.
However, it's what everyone else is doing.

"Lady" watching the boys ride their hot wheels.
First, they go down and then they go up the street.

I think I'll rest while I watch the boys.
Maybe I can get a little sunbathing in too!!!

Shawn's Best Friend "Lady" in Billings, Montana
(Where a boy is, his dog is)

Watching the boys play in the back yard
After a hard day of watching, them ride their bikes.

You know there is unconditional love when your dog won't come in out of the heat because she wants to be with the kids at play.

Chapter 6 "Missy "

The boys and I had been on our own for several years. However, I missed "Lady" and not having a dog around especially since I lived in a place where I had no friends or family. We were in the habit of visiting the pet store as we had done it for years. One year right before Christmas we walked into the Pet Store and there was this beautiful Australian Shepard puppy. We all fell in love with her. I told the boys it would be part of their Christmas present, as we didn't have much money. They agreed and we left with a new dog. We named her "Missy". She was black and white. Her ears were black but the majority of her body was white. She was as smart as a whip but needed some training. She was only a couple months old and it would take some work getting her to listen and follow directions. She was pretty well house broke but would have an occasional accident from having been kept in a cage at the pet store. I put newspaper on the floor and I taught her to bark when she wanted out. She was a working dog and I had warned the boys never to fight in front of her, as she liked to nip at the heels. However, boys being boys one day they got into a physical fight in the house and she didn't like it. The next thing we knew "Missy" had grabbed my youngest son, who was around eleven years old, at the time, by the seat of his pants and drug him down the hall to protect him from his older brother. It made him mad as it put a hole in his pants but didn't break the skin. Both of the boys were surprised but I had to laugh because I had warned them and they hadn't listened. "Missy" didn't like it if anyone raised their voice or there was any kind of confrontation. "Missy" was a dog of high energy and she liked to work so it was important to keep her busy. She liked being put on a leash and taken for walks and she enjoyed going for a ride in the car. She traveled well when we went out of town. We would soon move to a smaller town and find ourselves living in small houses. Now we didn't have a fenced yard so whenever she went outside someone would have to be with her. Our house was small and there wasn't much room for everyone and our furniture so we made the best of it that we could. "Missy" loved to be with my youngest son as he was home the most and she would become attached to him. Eventually, I was able to find a better home for us but the problem was they would not permit any animals. We were living in a rural community where no one wanted to rent to pets. I talked it over with the boys and we decided it was in everyone's best interest to find a good home for "Missy" so that we could have a house that was good for all of us. It was the hardest thing I did but I found a nice couple that lived in Soda Springs where she'd have her own yard to run around in and they took her. I would often think of her and miss her. I had been raised an animal is family and I felt like I had betrayed her by giving her away. However, my children had to come first. We would only stay in our home that we had moved to for one year before there were problems with the landlord who I didn't trust. Then we would move again having a yard and a nice place to live. This would change everything for us. I wish that I had kept "Missy" however, I knew where she was she had a big yard and plenty of room to roam and could be a good dog for her new owners.

"Missy" I love you and hope your life was good.

Scared new puppy.

I'm a good listener.

I'm not very big and I don't need much!

I'm starting to get bigger is that okay?

*Shawn is teaching me to fetch that round thing.
I think he calls it a ball.*

Time for some Loving!

Mom, Shawn, and "Missy"
playing with her favorite toy.

Now they'll play with me and I can run.

Michael is it time to come out yet?

Michael I'm coming out ready or not!!!

Michael playing with "Missy" as Grandma watches.

"Missy" looking to see what's happening.

Time to rest.

Michael, Grandma, and "Missy"
getting out of the car to stretch.

Chapter 7 "China, Shadow and Puppies"

My youngest son came home one day and said, "Mom, I need to talk to you." I wondered what was going on as this was unusual. I sat down to listen to what he had to say but to my surprise, it wasn't what I expected. He said, that a friend of his had some pups that were going to the pound if she didn't find a home in the next couple of days. Now I knew how hard that would be in our community and I knew what the pound meant. I didn't want to hear this as I still wasn't over "Missy," but my baby boy who was growing into a nice young man had come to me with a problem and I wanted to be there for him. I told him how I felt and I said I wouldn't make any promises but to bring a couple of the female pups to the house after school and I'd take a look and see what we could do. That was my first mistake. He brought the pups, he was in love with one dog, and I feel in love with the other dog. Now my heart was saying I couldn't let these dogs go to the pound. We had a yard but it wasn't fenced and it would mean having to put them on chains when left outside. However, we ended up with both dogs. They were "Heinz 57" dogs. "China" looked like her mother and had some cocker spaniel in her. "Shadow" was a cross between a border collie, Shepard, blue heeler mix. "China" looked a lot like my dog, "Heidi," she was brown and white. She would frequently walk into walls and bump into things. I believe she had a vision problem but no one agreed with me. "Shadow" was grey with a marble effect, skinny, and full of energy. She wanted to play all the time. After having them for a couple of days "Shadow" got very sick and ended up at the Vet's with Parvo and almost died. It was costly and I was worried. However, "Shadow" had a will to live and ended up coming home healthy. "China" fortunately never got sick. However, both dogs were given immunizations and seen regularly by my Vet. We would spend a lot of time training two opposite dogs and we would frequently have to separate them during training time. Eventually, they learned what they were suppose to and became very good dogs. Things were going well except for one bad habit. "Shadow" liked to dig holes in the yard when left outside too long. Now that would upset my landlord. However, I would work with him on it and we survived his wrath. Nevertheless, we never were able to break her from digging. Things appeared to be going well until one day my oldest son who no longer lived at home showed up and he had a "Chow" with him, which was a male. Now my dogs had not been spayed yet due to finances. The next thing we knew "Shadow" was pregnant and we would have to deal with puppies. I had never in my life had a dog that had puppies and I didn't know what I was going to do as most of my time was spent at school working. I told my youngest son that he would be responsible for watching the dogs when they were out since he was the one who wanted to help his friend out and he agreed. When the time came for "Shadow" to have her puppies, my son had come home from school to check on her and if I remember correctly, she had already had the first one. Then she continued to have them. By the time, I arrived home from work there were five puppies. My son was outside assisting with each one as it arrived. "Shadow" was very trusting of us and would let us near them.

She was a good mother and things couldn't have gone better. However, I knew I would now have to find homes for these puppies. When the time came to wean them from their mother I ran an ad in the newspaper and we were able to find homes for all but one so we ended up keeping one of the pups. Now we had three dogs. I don't remember what we named the puppy however, the puppy looked like "Shadow." Life was changing around our home and I was now married and we were about to move to Las Vegas. My youngest son was about to get his first apartment and once again I was faced with what to do with the dogs. I knew I couldn't take them to Las Vegas with me and this broke my heart once again. My husband wasn't fond of animals in the house in the first place and that added stress to the situation. Michael certainly couldn't take one to a small bachelor's apartment so now I had to find homes for them. I once again advertised and found a home right away for "Shadow" and her pup where they could be together on a farm with plenty of room to run. Now I had to worry about "China." I didn't want to give "China" to anyone as I still worried about her sight. My girlfriend agreed to take her and had a doghouse for her and would allow her in the house and take care of her. However, one day she was put out in the yard, off her chain, out in the country and was hit by a vehicle. Thus, sadly ended "China's" life. "China" I am so sorry that wasn't what I wanted for you. I never heard anything more about "Shadow" and her pup so I hope that they lived a good and happy life. Now as much as I love dogs I can't bring myself to have one because I don't want to go through another loss of a dog.

I have loved and cared for each one of them as if they were my own babies and I have cried over each one. I will enjoy someone else's dogs but my time for having a dog is past.

**"China "cooling of on the sidewalk.
My human comes out to spend time with me**

I get to run around the yard with no chain on while my humans are outside with me. I love my yard!

*"Auntie China" will supervise the babies while mom
gets a break after having her batch of pups.
Shadow resting close by.*

*"China" alert to everything; responding to her name
while watching the pups.*

One Pup

Two Pups

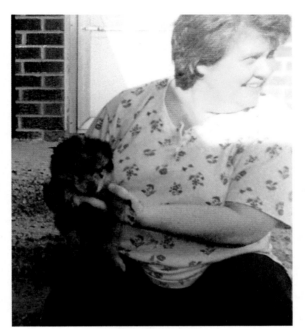

Three Pups

Four Pups

Five Pups

No wonder "Shadow" is so tired. "Shadow" was a small framed dog and dad was a full size "Chow Mix" dog.

Time to cool off on the cement near the water.

Nap Time!

Puppies playing in the yard while being watched.

Janice giving "Shadow" and "puppies"
some needed attention

Chapter 8 "Family Dogs"

Throughout the years, the family has had a variety of dogs ranging from terriers, cocker spaniels, collies, retrievers, and Heinz 57. Aunts and uncles, grandparents, sisters, children and now grandchildren have experienced the wonder of living with "Man's Best Friend." One thing that my entire family has always believed is that if you bring an animal into your life you are responsible for that animal. It becomes part of your family, and should be treated as such. Dogs have been spoiled the same as children. Dogs should not be left outside to fight the elements or to worry about food and water. My family has learned that there are many good dogs that can be adopted from animal shelters. Then they are saved from a horrible life or being put to sleep. The one thing that I learned from my dogs is that no matter whether I had a good day or a bad day my dog always showed me unconditional love and affection. There is nothing better than having a dog run to meet you when you come home after a long day of work. Although I no longer have dogs I still love them and will continue to support those who love and care for their animals. Remember children need to be taught how to love an animal. Don't just assume that they will automatically know how to treat an animal correctly. They live by what they are taught. Teach your children compassion for all animals and the world will be a better place. I know my life was better by having dogs in it. My biggest regret was having to give up several of my dogs in order to survive. However, I always tried to make sure they had a good home to move.

Fred Jr. (my dad) with the family dog.

Fred Jr. as a boy with his Springer Spaniel.

Fred Jr. with his dog "Tiny"

Fred Senior with the family dog in the country.

Dogs were part of the family and they went wherever the family went whether it was hunting, fishing, camping, or on a vacation. Your dog was at your side.

Hi! My name is "Kayaus" (Chaos). I belong to Aunt Barbara and Uncle Daniel. I am always ready for any attention that you give me. I am a German Shorthaired Retriever. I love to go hunting. I have to be careful because I am allergic to everything in the environment so my humans spend extra time seeing that I am cared for and eat the right type of food. I am an excellent hunting dog.

This is "Rambo" and "Kayaus" at mealtime.

Here is "Kayaus" retrieving from a nice dip in the water.

Daniel and I like to bird hunt.

I have to keep in shape retrieving
for when we go hunting.

Why's it so dark in here????

Chapter 9 "Why Dogs Bark"

Dogs are like people they have a lot to say. They want to communicate with humans. They do it by barking. They bark it to let you know what they want whether it is to go out, or come in, they also bark to warn you when there are strangers and other animals near. Dogs also bark when they don't like a person. Animals are known for being a good at judge of a person's character.

However, too much barking or barking at inappropriate times becomes a problem. It is important for any dog owner to have the barking under control, not only to respect the laws and rights of your neighbour but also to have a strong relationship between dog and owner.

Some Common causes of barking:

Attention/Demand: Your dog may want to be fed, go outside, or need your undivided attention. Dogs are social animals and need social interaction. Dogs that are left alone all the time become depressed and will do anything for interaction.

Boredom/Frustration: Dogs left alone whether outside or inside for long periods will bark for attention. Dogs are easily frustrated if alone for long periods. Most breeds have been breed for certain duties and they have the need to be busy.

Fear: Your dog may have a fear of objects, people, places, other animals, or loud noises such as thunder and fireworks. It may have been abused at some time. This is also common if children tease a dog walking by the yard especially if they have a stick and poke inside of the dog's territory.

TIP: Your dog's posture can tell you if he is barking out of fear. Typically, his ears go back, and his tail is held low. This is frequently seen when the dog bonds with only one family member and is scolded by another. It is important that all members of the family bond with your dog.

Territoriality/Protectiveness: Your dog is barking in the presence of "intruders," which may include people and other dogs in adjacent yards. Remember a dog never forgets a scent, so if it has been attacked before it will recall that scent if near.

TIP: If your dog is being territorial, his posture appears threatening with his tail held high and his ears up and forward. A simple command can relax your dog.

Playfulness/Excitement: Your dog may become overly playful and excited when greeting people often leading to jumping and barking at the same time. It is important to be in control of your dog at that time to keep everyone safe including your animal.

Health Issues: *Dog's may have Canine Cognitive Dysfunction or deafness, which will cause him to bark because he's not able to hear himself. Any time a dog cannot be in control of his territory, he will become nervous. It is important to use hand signals with this type of dog. They respond to simple hand signals if trained early.*

Dealing with health-related barking: *Some dogs bark because of age-related dementia or deafness. It is important to keep his environment simple and orderly; don't make frequent changes. Be patient with your dog and learn to teach him hand signals and flashlight commands. Dogs are not different from people; the older we become the more we want stability in our lives.*

Dealing with multiple barking dogs: *If you share your home and your life with more than one dog, you know how they can set each other off. Each dog must be trained individually. However, they can accomplish the ability to know when to bark and when to stop by your commands. Then everyone will be happy. Having more than one animal can be a challenge in the beginning until they are trained. They are company for each other and have better social adjustment because they look out for each other.*

Chapter "10 Tips for Petting a Dog"

How you pet a dog will determine your long-term relationship with him/her. It can make you the beloved human that is greeted, and anxiously looked forward to, or it can make you the person of apprehension to avoid.

Proper Greeting:
First Never **pet a dog that doesn't initiate a pet.** *This is very important for children to understand.*

Squat down *so that you are at his level instead of just reaching out and touching the dog.*

Turn your body to the side *to make yourself less threatening with a dog that is reserved or fearful. With a more confident dog, you can invite him to approach by bending over slightly patting your legs and backing up while coaxing with your voice.*

Avoid hovering *over the dog while greeting him. This can be interpreted as a threatening environment. Make minimal eye contact at first and allow the dog to approach you first. With a shy dog, it is best to pretend to ignore him and look away for the first few moments until he feels safe enough to approach you. Once the approach has been made then you want to pet the dog slowly in areas where he is comfortable being touched. A dog that enjoys being petted will usually lean toward the person or actively seek contact when you stop petting him.*

If the dog moves away or displays signs of discomfort, such as licking his lips or showing the whites of his eyes, it is time to give him his space.

Best Spots to Pet:
Chest
Shoulders
Base of the Neck

It is best not to reach over the top of the head but move from side to side.
Some dogs have special spots they like to be Pet; such as the base of the tail, under the chin, and on the back of the neck where the collar hits.

Most dogs dislike:
The muzzle area, ears, legs, paws, and tail. This may change once the dog is secure with his owner.
Slow petting similar to a gentle massage can often calm a dog down. Place your hand on an area where the dog enjoys being handled and with gentle motions move your hand or fingers in the same directions that the fur lays. Petting should be a calming enjoyable experience for both the animal and the person. **When you do this in a gentle manner, he is more likely to lean in for more.**

Petting Don'ts:

Patting by small children
Slapping a dog's side in excitement
Vigorous, fast or hard petting
Any of these can make the dog uncomfortable, causing agitation, excitement or overestimation of the animal.

When a dog rolls over on his stomach, beware: *this is a threatening position usually used to hold off another dog. That is not the time to pet your dog.*

Hugs hinder movement: *dogs like to feel safety within their own space. They don't like restriction of their movements.*

Don't put your face in a dogs face: *especially for children- this is threatening and a dog may protect itself.*

NEVER: Pet a dog that is
Chained up
Behind a barrier
Fenced
Inside a car

When a dog is trapped: *he is more likely to bite for self-protection.*

Never put a dog on a leash without permission from the animal's owner.

Chapter "11 Dog Behaviors"

Who is running the show you or your dog?
If your dog sees you as the alpha then you will be treated with respect and obedience of rules and commands. This relationship has to be developed and earned. It is a sign of respect in the relationship.

A Submissive dog *may express itself by licking the faces of the leaders, showing their delicate lower stomach regions. It may do this by keeping its body near the floor while avoiding eye contact if possible.*
.

Pawing *in both young puppies and adult doggies alike indicate an invitation for playtime rather than dominance. Pawing is usually a common form of rough play displayed among young puppies, along with pouncing, chasing and other similar behaviors. Sometimes it carries over into adulthood especially if the puppy was weaned prematurely from its mother.*

Pawing *can be a curious behavior too. Pawing at you can mean there is something fascinating to learn about whether it is the texture of a material or the movement of an object.*

Pawing *is very similar to toddlers touching everything to experience new items.*

Both Paws on You

When a dog is extremely tactile with you, whether pushing his body against you or pawing at you, it usually is a sign that he sees himself as being in control of his interactions with you. Don't miss read this signal for affection. Plenty of personal space is a determined factor of the utmost esteem in the hierarch of the canine world.

Typical dominant Patterns are:
Mounting
Growling
Snarling
Lack of regard for commands
Jumping up and Down on Furniture
Protective Behaviors of toys, food and prized possessions.

Professional Animal trainers are wise in the case of an aggressive behavior with your dog.

VOCALIZATIONS

Dogs will communicate in many different ways for many different reasons. Some of there ways of communicating are the following:

Howl: *This usually comes because of Loneliness*
Growl: *This is usually a signal of warning, or disgust*
Barking: *One bark is usually a call-out (hey!). Multiple barks in rapid succession is an alarm, or an effort to rally the social group to investigate something it finds interesting or threatening. Barking begins with a yodel or howl, it maybe an excited alert, or an alarm.*
Moan: *Is usually an intense pleasure or contentment*

Whine: This is usually begging or a signal that I want something. It frequently starts low and ends high. Your dog may be begging or asking for something. Sounds that start high and end low are usually signals of unhappiness, or a complaint.

Multiple Even-Pitch Grumbles: (wa, wa, wa, wa) This is usually wanting, asking, frustration or discontent sounds. In other words, we need attention.

Multiple High-Pitch Grumbles/whines-combo: We are Defending, or complaining about something, we aren't happy about.

High-Pitched Barking: We are saying come on and play or we are frustrated

Yawn (vocalized): This usually demonstrates excitement or frustration. This is also a calming signal. It also is a stress reducer of personal stress levels or stress levels in a social group. Commonly observed at vet's office, groomer, and before walks (excitement).

SILENT SIGNALS:

Turning away of the head: This is usually a calming signal. It means we have peaceful intentions. This is a time when the dog is avoiding potential conflict. A dog will prevent making direct eye contact (which many dogs consider a threatening behavior).

Lip licking: *This is recognized as a peaceful intention. It is a calming signal. This signal calms members of a social group, eases tension in a group or personal stress; it may precede a bite in a fearful dog, or precede presenting the belly.*

Shaking: *(This is exactly what a dog looks like after a bath when shaking off the water.) This is a stress reliever. You may encounter this after your dog has a scary or very exciting experience.*

Tail positions:

When **Elevated:** *It is usually a sign of confidence.*

Over back: *Is a sign of extreme confidence or dominance.*

Down: *Shows a relaxed, submissive animal.*

Betweenlegs: *The animal is fearful.*

Wagging with entire body/hips: *This is a sign of happiness.*

Wagging without body: *The animal is stressed, interested, feels aggression, or excitement, the dog is thinking.*

Hooked tail pointed downward: *Now we have excitement (commonly observed in Foxhounds, Basset Hounds, some Beagles or hunting animals).*

Piloerection (raised hackles): The dog now feels threatened. It is a signal of over-stimulation, or excitement.

Shivering: This is a dog's way of communicating fear, tension, or over-stimulation. When mammals, are confronted with a stressful event, their core body temperature raises, causing stress-induced hyperthermia.

Kissing of the Mouth: (Dog licking the mouth of a dog, or a human) this is puppy behavior. It is a sign of peaceful intentions, or submissive behavior. It is recognized as one of the most common reasons dogs jump during greeting rituals.

Blinking: Is known as a calming signal, peaceful intentions, or sleepiness.

Paw lift: When a dog shows **weight distribution toward the front of the body** this is a signal of peaceful intentions, or begging.

When it demonstrates weight distribution toward the rear of the body: This is a sign of fearful, distrustful, or unsure behavior.

Smile: Is when the jaw muscles are relaxed, and the tongue is exposed. There is no visible crease on the face, or forehead.

Closed Mouth: *This is a warning and usually precedes a bite. It is a way of gaining better scent; conveying seriousness, and thinking about the animals' actions.*

Open Mouth: *A dog with an open mouth is usually very relaxed.*

Grimace: *(Often referred to as a fear grimace, but also seen in excited dogs) this is when you see the dog with tense jaw muscles. The mouth is pulled back at the corners exposing molars or all of his/her teeth. When there are visible creases at corners of mouth, forehead it is usually a sign of fear, tension, or excitement. A forced smile look may be an exhibit of tension and fear.*

Whale Eye: *White of eyes visible with dilated pupils is a sign of fear, or aggression.*

Averted Gaze: *This is usually a sign of peaceful intentions, polite behavior, or fear.*

Staring: *When at an object the dog is usually claiming, or has intent to claim. When it is at another dog the animal is challenging the other. This may be for social status to prove which dog is dominant. A dog will also use this technique with a human to determine dominance.*

Presenting the Belly: *When an animal is laying squarely on his/her back, with floppy paws over center of chest, this is a sign of submission, or trust. When the dog is on its side, lifting one hind leg or one front paw (or both) this is a signal of fear, apprehension, fearful submission, or uncertainty. Urinating while doing either shows excitement or fear (submissive urination). This is a puppy behavior that some adult dogs will engage in when over-excited or fearful. It is a way to convey puppy-like intentions and that it isn't a threat.*

Sneeze: *Often takes place during enjoyable activity and laughter. (It may also happen when sniffing pepper).*

Bowing: *This is a sign that your animal is playful.*

Breathing: *When your animal is breathing through the stomach this is a sign of being relaxed. However, when breathing through the chest it is a sign of being excited.*

Panting: *This is a sign that your animal is either cooling the body down, excited, or in fear. The environment will usually tell you which one.*

Scraping Earth with Paws after Elimination: *This signals insecurity, marking territory for other dogs to see. It is using both elimination and its sweat glands on its paws.*

Sweaty Paws: *This is a signal that your dog is overheated, fearful, or stressed. It is often observed in the crates of dogs that have fear of confinement.*

Sniffing Ground: *This signals that your dog is in a state of calmness, and has peaceful intentions. It is a stress reliever.*

Freezing: *When your dog demonstrates this it is contemplating fight or flight, it is a warning. Your animal has reached a point of reactivity/threshold.*

Drooling: *This may be a signal of presence of food demonstrating hunger. It may also be stressful situations showing fear. Often precedes vomiting.*

If you don't understand your dog, behavior, ask a Vet for a professional opinion.

Chapter 12 "Important Dog Behaviors"

Dog behavior can be very confusing to both new and experienced dog owners. Dogs do not operate with the same motivations as people, so their actions don't always make sense to us. Have you ever wondered about your dog's behavior, and how you may be affecting it?

Here are ten most common dog behavior issues. They explain how to resolve them in every dog owners home.

Chewing:
Puppies love to chew, especially while they are teething. It feels good on raw gums, and very young puppies use their mouths to explore their world, tasting as they. This is very similar to what a baby would do when teething.

This is both natural and unavoidable, so prevention is necessary.

Dog proof your home by moving harmful items just like you would baby proof it. Check the following items especially wires, power cords, cleaning supplies, and other small objects that will need to be out of your dog's reach.

You can never have too many acceptable chew toys on hand.

Give your puppy a favorite chew toy that is agreed on by everyone. Such as an old worn out slipper that becomes your dogs. That will avoid chewing on good shoes. Play frequently with your dog and its toys so it understands that it is acceptable.

For teething puppies, freeze a baby's teething ring or even a knotted rag for quick, inexpensive relief. When your dog has sufficient acceptable toys to chew, he will not chew on unacceptable items.

There are commercial spray products available to put on items you don't want chewed on by your dog. These sprays will make anything taste unpleasant. If you choose to use these sprays, test a small corner of the item first to avoid ruining it.

Although this method can be effective, it should only be used to supplement the addition of acceptable chew toys. Spraying your personal items with bitter spray won't teach your dog to chew on only his toys. Training your dog is the best answer for everyone's happiness and safety.

There should always be chew toys wherever your dog is whether it is a room or his/her crate. If you see your dog chewing on something, correct him by saying "No," and give him one of its toys instead. Remember you are teaching your puppy just as you would a child. Speak in a firm but not yelling manner. One-word commands are best.

Biting:

Biting is a natural part of healthy, friendly puppy play between animals. However, it is not a healthy part of puppy play with its owner.

Puppies learn when and how hard to bite by playing with their littermates; mimic this play by whining pitifully if your puppy bites you. Replace your hand with a chew toy and lavish praise on your puppy when it chews on the designated toy you have given to your puppy.

If your puppy keeps biting you, stand up, stop playing, and walk away. It is no fun unless someone is playing, and your dog will soon learn to stop chewing. For an older dog, correct by saying "No," withdraw your hand.

Never put up with a puppy biting or nipping you. A biting puppy will only have behavioral problems when it grows into adulthood.

If you are unable to train your puppy, find an obedience class; make sure that it has a good reputation, or talk to your Vet for further information.

Growling over food:

Many people think that dogs are entitled to be protective of their food and that growling is a natural response.

A dog growling at a person over food can escalate into much larger issues, especially if growling is just one of many other behavioral problems.

Place several small bowls of food next to each other. As your dog goes to eat one of the bowls, move one of the other bowls to the other side, but still within the dog's reach.

Keep up this repetition until the dog realizes that a human hand is no threat to his food.

You can also use a firm command as you do this so that the dog knows who is in control.

Under no circumstance, allow a child around a dog growling over food.

Barking:

Each time your dog barks, go see why the dog is barking.

If it is for a good reason, like a stranger near your property, praise the dog and then tell him to be quiet. If it is for another reason, like a squirrel in a tree, tell the dog to be quiet and immediately go back into the house.

The dog will soon see that sometimes barking is acceptable, but not always. The dog will learn to bark for the right reasons.

If the dog sees a squirrel in a tree, he will still bark, but not continually. Instead, he will bark once or twice to scare the squirrel and be satisfied.

After all, he is stating that it is his territory. Once your dog is comfortable in the setting and knows it is his territory it will be much easier to give a one-word command.

Digging:

Dogs like to make dens whether out of boredom, or to make a nice spot to lie down. Digging is a natural tendency for dogs.

If you have the room to do so, make an acceptable spot for your dog to dig. A dirt spot at the bottom of the yard is good. An area that is cool in the summer and warm in the winter. Periodically turn the dirt over or place new earth in order to keep it exciting for your pet.

If you don't have room, fill the holes your dog makes with rocks, sticks, dead leaves, pine needles, or even old dog feces.

The dog will find this junk when he digs and quit digging, with the idea that it is not worth the effort to dig if nothing interesting comes out of it.

You can also place your dog's toys or treats in a box and encourage your dog to dig in it by digging in the space yourself. This works especially well for housedogs.

No matter whether an indoor or outdoor dog, it is important to remember that your pet has the instinct to dig.

Getting in the Garbage:

If a dog is trained correctly and you have house proofed everything this will not be a problem. However if your dog has a tendency to get into the garbage then here are some helpful tips that you might want to follow:

Crate the dog to keep him out of the garbage when you're not home, and correct the dog when he gets into the garbage while you are at home.

Purchase a heavy-duty lidded step trashcan and take it out before it becomes overflowing or a problem.

Dispose of especially savory trash immediately, like bones and meat.

Never allow your dog at the table during mealtime.

We always fed our dog at the same time we ate. This avoided problems of them wanting to beg for food or bother family members or guests while eating a meal.

Jumping is a dog's expression of happiness:

If you do not mind your dog jumping, train your dog to jump only when it is ok, via a signal that you give your dog. Otherwise, it will equate jumping as an always-okay action. This can become challenging when guests that do not own dogs come to visit your home. Keep in mind not everyone will find this behavior an acceptable behavior and it is important your dog knows the time and place to do it.

Keep in mind that a dog jumping can harm an elderly person. There needs to be protection not only for children but also for the elderly or those physically fragile.

Correct the dog immediately when he is about to jump.

Praise him when all four paws are back on the ground.

Soiling in the house:

Even dogs that are housebroken make mistakes. This can happen for a variety of behavioral or emotional reasons.

If your dog has a physical problem like a urinary tract or parasite infection, he will lose control of his bladder.

Some dogs temporarily lose control of their bladders when they become excited, feel threatened or are scared.

Dogs also mark their territory with urine; if they believe their territory has been invaded, they may incite territorial markings.

Dogs may also make mistakes in the house because of separation anxiety. If they are left alone in the house for long periods, and soiling is accompanied by other destructive behavior, then separation anxiety is likely the cause.

Identify the cause of the behavior and alter the environment so that he will not repeat the behavior.

Keep in mind that animals can catch the same diseases that humans do and have the same bodily functions.

When in doubt talk to a Vet.

Pulling on the leash:

The dog that does not walk properly on a leash requires training.

When the dog is about to apply any tension to the leash, immediately stop in your tracks and be firm.

When the dog turns to see what has happened to you, praise him for noticing, simultaneously move him back into his heel position, and continue walking with the heel command..

So long as the dog remains next to your leg, continue to praise him and give him rewards if necessary.

Right next to you should be the most fun place for him to be.

If he loses concentration and is about to put any tension on the leash again, stop without warning and repeat the sequence.

Using the Heel Command is recommended.

Whining or Crying:

This usually results from an owner giving in when a dog whines or cries. This provides positive reinforcement for the dog's actions. Dogs learn that whining produces a favored response from the owner. When the dog sees that if he whines, he gets a nice long walk, he will continue to whine in order to get what he/she wants from their owner.

Make sure your dog gets plenty of exercise, and is fed a healthy diet.

Reward him when his whining has stopped for over three seconds.

Ignore whining for attention at all costs.

Having a regular routine for walking and exercising your animal will help you to break this habit.

Effective Dog Discipline:

Remember that a dog is a pack animal, and he sees himself as part of your pack. However, dominance of the pack must be determined by you, so that the dog listens and obeys.

Once you cater to the dog's whim and let him lead, you become part of his pack and he becomes alpha male.

These common dog behaviors are easily trained out of a dog, so don't be alarmed if they're present in your puppy. Be consistent and firm when your dog does the wrong things, and keep the praise flowing when he does the right things.

Training your dog can be a process, but the happiness you'll gain from proper dog behavior makes the effort worthwhile.

Are You A Dog Person?

Are you thinking about getting a dog? Do you have an interest in understanding the differences in dog breeds and what dog behavior could be telling you? Some people dote on their canine friends, lavishing them with edible delicacies and cultured salon services. Others take a casual approach with pet care, viewing dogs as pets that are easily manipulated. Remember your animal is no different from a child it requires love, consistency and stability. You after all are the teacher and they are the student.

Chapter 13 "Dog Routines"

If you are a dog lover, your four-legged friend is your ultimate companion. But when you're feeling overwhelmed, you barely have time to exercise yourself, let alone make sure your new companion gets enough exercise, too. However, it is important to keep yourself and your dog healthy and happy with a few well-placed additions to your dog-care schedule.

Taking 20-to-30 minutes to walk your dog before tackling your next project can give you just what you need to clear your mind and get pumped up to move forward.

Walking your dog enforces a strong leadership position with your pet. You will find that for most dogs, trotting around by themselves in the backyard can be rather boring

Dogs crave love and attention and thrive on an established routine. This is especially important in terms of potty breaks and feeding times. Dogs need enough sleep to function effectively. When possible, consider designating an area of the house, such as a cushion or crate, for your dog, and keep your own bed a dog-free zone. This will allow your pet to have some ownership of his own special space and will ensure that you get a full night's sleep as well.

As part of your pup's schedule, try incorporating a 10-minute block of training time every day.

Don't stress about you or your dog performing perfectly. Make it a fun activity to break up your day, and an opportunity for a much-needed bonding time.

When your dog masters some of the common commands, you may be surprised how his overall behavior improves, too.

Now that you have a playful, obedient, well-fed pup, you'll want to show off your pride and joy. Make sure your dog's well groomed and that you keep up on necessary hygiene needs. Most dogs are pretty good self-groomers, but it's important that you keep up on monthly flea and tick care and perform maintenance on their nails, eyes and ears as needed. This can be done by establishing a grooming routine. Now, grab the leash, pick up that brush, or fill up that food bowl! However, most of all have fun! Your beloved dog is waiting for you!

1. Food & Water. How often will you **feed your dog**? Vets often recommend once or twice a day but some people feed outdoor/competing dogs as much as three times a day. Ask your vet how much food a day your dog should be given. Then simply divide these between the number of meals. Do not over- feed, as this will cause serious harm to your dog's health. Always feed according to your set routine, as this will keep your dog healthy. It will also make it much easier for you to predict when your dog will need a bathroom break.

*2. **Bathroom Breaks.** When and how much your dog eats will affect this. The following times are a **MUST** for every dog: **let your dog out after finishing every meal, after walks, after excessive play, when you wake up, and when you go to bed.** When your dog just needs to let a little extra out, he or she will bend his/her back legs, raise the tail straight in the air, and will curve his/her bottom. Follow your dog's bathroom routine.*

*3. **Cleaning and Accessories.** Ask your vet about how often your dog should be bathed. Your dog, no matter what breed, needs to be bathed once every four months. Regular baths depend on the breed, skin characteristics, fur length, fur coarseness, and sometimes age. You can get special shampoo for your dog at a vet or dog breed club. After each bath, brush your dog thoroughly, and do not rush. Get your dog comfortable with brushing. If your dog is an indoor dog with fine hair, a brushing once every day, in the morning, is recommended. Otherwise, occasional brushing won't hurt anybody. Remember you are interacting with your animal and it is important this is a pleasant experience for both of you.*

4. Play and Exercise. *Dogs need to play and exercise every day regardless of the weather. Play with your pet by running around, chasing it, tossing a small ball, but make sure the ball is not so small it can choke on it. You can also get a short thick length of rope and play tug of war. Make sure you are friendly while playing. If your dog gets a bit too playful and nips at you, say in* **a low-pitched tone, "no!"** *Sound firm but not angry, as you don't want to scare your dog, simply to correct the dog's behavior. If you don't have a back yard then you definitely need to walk your dog for at least an hour a day, every day. Without sufficient exercise, dogs become more restless and unhappy which will increase discipline problems.*

5. Social Life. *Don't keep your pet to yourself! If you invite friends over, and they are comfortable with dogs, all of you should play! If you happen to see another dog with his owner on a walk, introduce your self and let the dogs sniff each other, and friendly greetings will be a sure sign that your dog is not in a canine depression. It is important for dogs to be receptive to those who visit your home so they must be socialized in order for the best experience for all involved.*

6. Confinement and special areas. *If your dog could damage furniture, keep him/her in your largest bathroom, or an empty backroom. Never put your dog in an area with small objects on the floor, a low trash can, or nails coming out of the floor/walls. Even small dogs can knock trashcans over and sniff out some left over food. Nails can be bitten and can damage the teeth perhaps ripping the tissue. Small objects can be eaten, without a very promising outcome. Always keep an open area for your dog to enjoy. A small sample carpet on hard wood floors becomes a special seat just for your dog. Put a blanket next to your couch or chair, if you don't allow him/her on the furniture. Make sure your pet understands where you want him/her to lay down. For a bed, you can get a small blanket, rip out the seams, and stuff the inside of the blanket with old clothes or stained pillows. This will make it very cozy, and you have an inexpensive bed for your pet. As dogs, get older they need more padding to lay on so make sure the bedding is clean and comfortable.*

7. Write it down. *Write down your routine. Put it in you wallet, on your refrigerator, or blow it up and put it in a frame in your bedroom. Get creative! Do what ever it takes to help you be consistent in your routine with your new family member. This will also assist you if you ever need a dog sitter.*

Chapter "14 Important Dog Commands"

Dog owners should know the importance of teaching their dogs training commands to communicate and train their dogs to have proper behavior. It is important to use simple one-word commands that they can easily understand and learn. Knowing these commands will not only help you communicate with your dog but will make life much easier and happier for both of you and your canine.

Some of the beginning most common commands:

Come
This is the **first and most important** command, which is usually taught together with his/her name. This command is vital to show that you have control of your dog and can retrieve him/her when other people or animals approach. It also is a way of keeping your pet out of harms way. This is one of the easiest commands to teach. It is one of the most important commands when controlling your dog.

Sit
Dogs who understand the "Sit" command are easier to manage. They are also less likely to misbehave by jumping on people, chasing animals or fighting with other dogs.

Stay

This can be **used in combination with commands "sit" or "down."** The command "stay" is useful to keep your dog out of harms way should he/she approach something it's not suppose to, or stop it from attempting to run across a busy street. **It is one of the most important commands to teach** although it may not be the easiest due to curiosity of the animal.

Wait

This should not be confused with the "Stay" command which is more often use to keep your dog away from danger. **The "Wait" command is more of obedience** commands to keep your dog in check, letting him/her know he/she has to wait until your next command. This command can be used when a dog gets too eager so that they understand they have to wait for you.

Down

Unlike the "sit" command, the **"down" command means your dog goes down on his/her stomach.** This command is an **essential part of dog etiquette.** It is also more comfortable than a sitting position when you want your dog to wait for a longer period of time.

Stand

This command tells your dog to **stop moving and be still**. It is often used when you are having a veterinarian do an examination of him/her or when you are having someone bath or groom your pet and it is important that they don't move in order to keep them any everyone else safe.

Okay

The **"Okay" command is use to release** your dog from a previous command.

No

"No" is usually use to discourage or break up **undesirable behavior** such as chewing, biting or jumping. This is an important command that you should teach your puppy from the beginning during early learning.

Off

The "Off" command is useful to teach your dog **to get off the furniture or people** they are tempted to jump up on.

Leave It

The **"Leave It"** is a command that applies to **inquisitive animals** that sometimes give into instincts while exploring their senses. It can keep them out of a lot of trouble.

Drop It

The **"Drop It"** command is necessary to get your dog to drop whatever is in their mouth . This command is useful when teaching your dog how to **"Fetch"**. It may help keep them from picking up something that is harmful to them.

Heel

"Heel" simply means that your dog will **walk on your left** without lagging behind or running ahead of you. Your dog needs to understand this command, A pet should never be allowed to pull you on the leash while going for walks. This command becomes very important if you have a large dog.

Chapter "15 Feeding Your Canine"

Each individual dog has its own needs. An individual dog's requirements may differ from this chart. It is always best to consult with your vet about the specific needs of your pet.

First Eight weeks:

Puppies should never be separated from their mother before they are 8 weeks old. Puppies that leave their mothers sooner have a rougher time adjusting and run the risk of a higher incidence of illnesses. This could be because of a weakened immunity or mourning the premature loss of their family.

Their mother's milk provides them with the nutrition and antibodies they need to be healthy dogs. At three to four weeks, puppies should begin eating some solid food. You can try mixing three parts food with one part water, or you can also use puppy replacement milk. This makes the food easier for the puppy to digest.

If your puppy is eating a little solid food before it leave its mother it will have an easier time adjusting to being weaned from the mother.
One way to tell if a puppy is ready to come home with you is if it prefers human company to its mom or siblings.

Six to Eight Weeks:

Puppies need to be feed 3-4 times a day. Puppies have different nutritional needs than adult dogs just as a baby does. It is important to choose a puppy food that provides the appropriate balance of nutrients. It is important to make sure that it is getting the right amount of protein and calcium, and the proper amount of calories. Always check the label to determine if you are feeding your puppy a balanced diet. A specified meat should be the first ingredient on the label

After Eight weeks:

You may start a routine of feeding your puppy twice a day.

Three to six months:

During this time, your puppy will be teething. He/she may become a finicky eater or lose his appetite. Keep your routine of feeding him nutritious food twice a day. If he has an upset stomach for more than one or two days, take him to the veterinarian.

Six months to one year:

Your puppy may look grown up but it is important to remember he is still a puppy. It is important to feed a high quality food for the added nutrition.

Note, in some very high quality foods the company does not make a separate food for puppies because the food is of such a high quality that it provides for both puppy and adult equally.

For example, a real human grade chicken is what it is for all ages. If you are feeding puppy food, ask your veterinarian when you should switch to adult food. Make sure the adult food you switch to is still a balanced high quality diet with the first ingredient being a specified meat that is not a by-product.

Eight to Nine Months:
Feeding should be twice a day continue a steady routine.

One year old:
 In most breeds feeding should be twice a day

Remember dogs like a routine that is consistent, and if you feed them when you eat, they are less likely to bother you at your mealtime.

However as your dog gets older it is necessary to talk with your Vet about when to make changes in dietary needs.

Chapter "16 Dog Myths and Facts"

Remember it is all about the health of the dog.

1. Dogs should have a litter before they are spayed.

This is not true. In fact, spayed dogs are at lower risk for breast cancer and uterine infections. Dogs that have a litter before they are spayed are not affected in any way

2. Dogs are sick when their noses are warm.

This is an "old wives tale" that a cold wet nose indicates health, and a warm or dry nose indicates a fever or illness. The temperature of a dogs nose does not indicate health or illness or if they have a fever. The only accurate method to access a dog's temperature is to take it with a thermometer. A dog's normal temperature is 100.5 to 102.5 degrees F.

3. Mutts are always healthier than purebred dogs.

This is not true. Both mutts and purebred dogs can be unhealthy. Both can have diseases. Mutts generally however, do not have some of the genetic diseases common in purebred lines.

4. All dogs like to be petted on their heads.

Some dogs do not like to be petted on their heads because they feel threatened. However, some do like it.

5. Happy Dogs Wag Their Tails.

*This may be true. However, aggressive dogs often wag their tails too. Several physical body movements and cues help dogs to communicate their intent. A wagging tail can mean agitation or excitement. A dog that wags his tail slowly and moves all his rear end or crouches down in the classic "play bow" position is usually a **friendly wag**. Tails that are wagged when held higher, twitches or tail wagging while held over the back may be related with **aggressive behaviour**.*

6. Only male dogs will "hump" or lift their leg to urinate.

This is not true. Dominant female dogs will lift their leg to urinate and "hump" other dogs or objects. This can be true even if they are spayed.

7. Table scraps are good for dogs.

Some table scraps such as bones and pieces of fat can be dangerous to some pets. They may not digest the bones and the fat may cause gastrointestinal problems such as pancreatitis. Dogs may also choke on bones such as chicken bones and should never be given bones that easily fracture.

8. Garlic prevents fleas.

Garlic has not been proven helpful for flea control. Large amounts of garlic can even be harmful to our canine friends.

9. Household "pet dogs" don't need to be trained.

This is not true. Every dog should be trained. Dogs need to be trained early as puppies and it is important for consistency.

10. Dogs eat grass when they are sick.

Dog descended from wild wolves and foxes that ate all parts of their "kill." This included the stomach contents of many animals that ate berries and grass. Many scientists believe grass was once part of their normal diet and eating small amounts is normal.

11. Dogs like tasty food.

Dogs have very poor taste buds and eat primarily based on their sense of smell. A dog is a very good judge of good food. You know if a dog won't eat it, you shouldn't either.

12. Licking is Healing.

It is natural for a dog to lick its wound but this is not necessarily always "healing." Too much licking can actually prohibit healing. In fact, too much licking can be a sign of other health problems and you should consult your Vet.

13. Dogs will let you know when they are sick.

This is not true. Dogs generally are very good at hiding that they are sick by survival instinct, thus not to appear vulnerable to "prey." Often by the time, they show you that they are sick, their disease or condition is quite advanced.

Dogs are also known for going off by themselves when sick and you may have to go looking for your canine friend and bring it home safely.

14. Indoor Dogs don't need heartworm prevention.

This is not true. Indoor pets are also at risk for heartworm disease. Heartworm disease is spread by mosquitoes, which can come inside. Have regular check ups with your Vet.

15. Dogs eat rocks, lick concrete or eat their or another animals stools because of nutrient imbalances.

No one knows why dogs eat "stuff" that they shouldn't eat. Some veterinarians believe that some dogs that eat "things" may be trying to get attention or acting out of boredom. It is important for dogs to eat a well balanced diet that will fulfil their dietary and nutrient requirements. It is just as important for you to spend time giving your animal the attention it deserves to keep it happy and reduce boredom.

16. Dogs don't need to be housebroken. They naturally know where to go.

You need to train your dog where to go. This preferably happens when you start young and give him positive encouragement for jobs well done. If you are consistent with this, both you and your pet will be happier.

Chapter "17" Dog Proverbs and Sayings

Proverbs:
Chinese Proverb

"One dog barks at something, the rest bark at him."

Danish Proverbs

"The dog's kennel is not the place to keep a sausage."
"An honest man is not the worse because a dog barks at him."

Dutch, Russian Proverb

"Barking dogs don't bite."

Egyptian Proverb

"The barking of a dog does not disturb the man on a camel."

English Proverb

"A dog that runs after two bones catches neither."

German Proverbs

"To live long, eat like a cat, drink like a dog."

Haitian Proverb

"Children aren't dogs; adults aren't Gods."

Indian Proverb

"Only mad dogs and Englishmen go out in the noonday sun."

Italian Proverb

"Those who sleep with dogs will rise with fleas."

Latin Proverb

"Beware of a silent dog and still water."

Moroccan, Jewish saying

"Do not respond to a barking dog."

Polish Proverb

"The greatest love is a mother's; then a dog's; then a sweetheart's.

Portuguese Proverb

"A house without either a cat or a dog is the house of a scoundrel."
"The dog wags his tail, not for you, but for your bread.

Russian Proverb

"If you are a host to your guest, be a host to his dog also."

Saudi Arabian Proverb

"If you stop every time a dog barks, your road will never end."

US Proverb

"A good dog deserves a good bone."
"Every dog is allowed one bite."

Welsh Proverb

"Three things it is best to avoid: a strange dog, a flood, and a man who thinks he is wise."

Yiddish Proverb

"Show a dog a finger, and he wants the whole hand."

Sayings:

"Dogs feel very strongly that they should always go with you in the car, in case the need should arise for them to bark violently at nothing right in your ear." -
Dave Barry

"A dog is one of the remaining reasons why some people can be persuaded to go for a walk."
OVA. Battista

"The dog was created specially for children. He is the God of frolic."
Henry Ward Beecher

"Dachshunds are ideal dogs for small children, as they are already stretched and pulled to such a length that the child cannot do much harm one way or the other."
Robert Benchley

"The most affectionate creature in the world is a wet dog."
Ambrose Bierce

"A dog is the only thing on earth that loves you more than you love yourself."
Josh Billings

*"The great pleasure of a **dog** is that you may make a fool of yourself with him and not only will he not scold you, but he will make a fool of himself too."*
Samuel Butler

"The nose of the bulldog has been slanted backwards so that he can breathe without letting go."
Winston Churchill

"The dog is a yes-animal, very popular with people who can't afford to keep a yes-man."
Robertson Davies

"Dogs laugh, but they laugh with their tails."
Max Eastman

"Properly trained, a man can be dog's best friend."
Corey Ford

"In order to really enjoy a dog, one doesn't merely try to train him to be semi-human. The point of it is to open oneself to the possibility of becoming partly a dog." - **Edward Hoagland**

"Anybody who doesn't know what soap tastes like never washed a dog."
Franklin P. Jones

"The pug is living proof that God has a sense of humor."
Margo Kaufman

"If you are a dog and your owner suggests that you wear a sweater... suggest that he wear a tail."
Fran Lebowitz

"No philosophers so thoroughly comprehend us as dogs and horses."
Herman Melvill

"Did you ever walk into a room and forget why you walked in? I think that is how dogs spend their lives."
Sue Murphy

"If you think dogs can't count, try putting three dog biscuits in your pocket and then giving Fido only two of them."
Phil Pastoret

"The best way to get a puppy is to beg for a baby brother - and they'll settle for a puppy every time."
Winston Pendelton.

"From the dog's point of view, his master is an elongated and abnormally cunning dog."
Mabel Louise Robinson

"*I love a dog. He does nothing for political reasons.*"
Will Rogers

"*The average dog is a nicer person than the average person.*"
Andy Rooney

"*I wonder if other dogs think poodles are members of a weird religious cult.*"
 Rita Rudner

"*Happiness is a warm puppy.*"
Charles M. Schulz

"*The more one gets to know of men, the more one values dogs.*"
Alphonse Toussenel

"*If you get to thinking you're a person of some influence, try ordering somebody else's dog around.*"
Will Rogers

"*There is no psychiatrist in the world like a puppy licking your face.*"
Ben Williams

"If a dog will not come to you after having looked you in the face, you should go home and examine your conscience."
Woodrow Wilson

"The reason a dog has so many friends is that he wags his tail instead of his tongue."
Author Unknown

"A dog can express more with his tail in seconds than his owner can express with his tongue in hours."
Author Unknown

Chapter "18 Ancient Dogs!"

Dogs have been part of human culture for 15,000 years.

All dogs descended from the gray wolf, the largest member of the Canidae family. (Copyright Staffan Widsrtrand/Nature Picture Library)

Today there are around some 77 million dogs in the United States alone. However, as late as 20,000 years ago, it's possible there wasn't a single animal on the planet that looked like today's Canis lupus familiaris. How and when the species first became recognizably "doggy" has puzzled scientists since the theory of evolution first gained acceptance in the 19th century. The original idea that dogs were once domesticated from jackals was long ago discarded with the belief that they were descendents from the grey wolf, Canis lupus. This is the largest member of the Canidae family, which includes foxes and coyotes. While no scholars seriously dispute this basic fact of ancestry of the history of dogs, many still debate when, where, and how grey wolves first evolved into today's dogs.

Where were the first dogs domesticated? Were they domesticated in China, the Near East, or possibly Africa? What was the reason that they were first bred? Were they first bred for food, companionship, or their hunting abilities? The answers are important, since dogs were the first animals to be domesticated and likely played a critical role in the Neolithic revolution.

Distinguishing between wolf and dog skeletons can be very difficult, especially early in the history of dogs, when they would have been much more similar to wolves than today's dogs.

Recently, biologists have debated, about when and where wolves first developed into what we today recognize as dogs.

What are perhaps the earliest dog-like remains date to 31,700 years ago and were excavated in the 19th century at Goyet Cave in Belgium. This dog-like wolf could represent the first step toward domestication and would make the Paleolithic people we call the Aurignacians, better known as the first modern humans to occupy Europe. These would be recognized, as the world's first known dog lovers. However, the analysis is controversial because there is a large gap between the age of the Goyet Cave "dog" and the next oldest skeletons that could possibly resemble dog like, dating to 14,000 years ago in western Russia. The Goyet Cave wolf perhaps is a representation of an isolated instance of what we consider domestication and left no descendants. We know that certainly 10,000 years ago dogs were playing a critical role in the lives of humans all over the world, based on finds of dog skeletons throughout the Old World, from China to Africa whether as sentries, ritual sacrifices, or sources of protein

If we explore roles of dogs played in past cultures throughout the world and how ancient artists celebrated humans oldest companions, we should be aware of the following

- **Constant Companions**

- **Sacrificial Dogs**

- **Dogs of Roman Britain**

- **Dogs as Food**

- **Catacombs of Dogs**

- **Guardians of souls**

The archaeological record suggests dogs were domesticated in multiple places through out different periods. A team led by Peter Savolainen, of the Royal Institute of Technology in Stockholm, published an analysis of the mitochondrial DNA of some 1,500 dogs from across the Old World in 2009. He narrowed down the time and place of dog domestication to a few hundred years in China. "He found that dogs were first domesticated at a single event, sometime less than 16,300 years ago, south of the Yangtze River," says Savolainen, who posits that all dogs spring from a population of at least 51 female wolves, which were first bred over the course of several hundred years."

This is the same basic time and place as the origin of rice agriculture," he notes.

"It's speculative, but it seems that dogs may have first originated among early farmers, or perhaps hunter-gatherers who were sedentary." A team led by biologist Robert Wayne of the University of California, Los Angeles, showed that domesticated dog DNA overlaps most closely with that of Near Eastern wolves. Wayne and his colleagues suggest that dogs were first domesticated somewhere in the Middle East, then bred with other grey wolves as they spread across the globe, casting doubt on the idea that dogs were domesticated during a single event in a discrete location. Savolainen maintains that Wayne overemphasizes the role of the Near Eastern Gray wolf, and that a more thorough sampling of wolves from China would support his team's theory of a single domestication event.

University of Victoria archaeozoologist, Susan Crockford, who did not take part in either study, suspects that searching for a single moment when dogs were domesticated overlooks the fact that the process probably happened more than once. "We have evidence that there was a separate origin of North American dogs, distinct from a Middle Eastern origin," says Crockford. "This corroborates the idea of at least two 'birthplaces.' I think we need to think about dogs becoming dogs at different times in different places."

As for how dogs first came to be domesticated, Crockford, along with many other scholars, thinks that dogs descend from wolves that gathered near the camps of semi-sedentary hunter-gatherers, as well as around the first true settlements, to eat scraps.

"The process was probably driven by the animals themselves," she says. "I don't think they were deliberately tamed; they basically domesticated themselves." Smaller wolves were probably more fearless and curious than larger, more dominant ones, and so the less aggressive, smaller wolves became more successful at living in close proximity to humans. "I think they also came to have a spiritual role," says Crockford. "Dog burials are firm evidence of that. Later, perhaps they became valued as sentries. I don't think hunting played a large role in the process initially. Their role as magical creatures was probably very important in the early days of the dog-human relationship."

Whatever the reasons behind the domestication of dogs, they have left their paw prints all over the archaeological record for thousands of years.

There is much additional information that one can review on the research of the dog heritage. If one is interested, I suggested that they spend time reading research studies and books that have been printed. I have simply given you a few quotes of where to find further information.

Wolf: The original dog: all dogs are believed to have come down line from. It is most likely that a population of wolves adopted humans rather than humans adopted them. As the advantages of dog ownership became clear, humans were as strongly affected by their relationship with wolves as they have been by their relationship with us. This may have been the beginning of our form of domesticated civilization. Wolves were known to run in packs and to be adequate hunters. They were smart and could be used not only for hunting but also as watchdogs. With humans and wolves being both carnivorous hunters, it came down to either living together or determining which one would become extinct. The choice was easy; it was much easier for humans to accept living together and utilizing their skills. Domesticated dogs were believed to have developed from wolves as they evolved due to survival of the fittest. Environment made them have adaptations in coloring, bodily characterizations and behaviors. Now we have many breeds of dogs, however, the ancient dogs started with those listed below.

- *Shar-pei:* *The Chinese Shar-Pei is recognized for his super wrinkly skin. The Shar-Pei was mainly used on Chinese farms and it performed a multitude of tasks such as guarding, catching rodents, herding, and tracking. These were a few of the skills they used in ancient times. The Chinese believed that these dogs would protect them from evil spirits. Today they are known for being intelligent but often stubborn.*

- *Shiba Inu:* *The Shiba Inu reminds one of little cute foxes and is down line from the Shar-pei. This breed comes from Japan where it was mainly a hunting dog. They were often bred to hunt in the heavy brush of the mountains. Their game included small animals, boar, and bear. These dogs are very small so one might wonder about them being used for bears. However, their size would allow them access to areas a human might not be able to get into.*

- *Chow Chow*: The *Chow Chow is a breed of dog that comes from China. It is down line from the Shar-pei. During ancient times, Chow Chows were used for a number of tasks including hunting, herding, pulling, and protection. They made excellent guard dogs*

- *Akita Inu: The breed originated from Japan. These dogs would track down animals like wild boar, deer, and even bears! They were also used as guard dogs.*

- **Basenji:** *Basenji is known as the breed that doesn't bark. It turns out that the Basenji breed is a dog that comes from Africa. In Africa, they were used as pointers, retrievers, and they aided hunters by directing their game into nets. They were brought to Pharaohs of ancient Egypt as presents. I didn't know much else about them.*

- **Siberian Husky:** *The Siberian Husky is thought to have originated on the Siberian peninsula where it's very cold. They have very thick double coats. In ancient times, they were used as sled dogs.*

- **Alaskan Malamute**: *Alaskan Malamutes were bred for endurance. They were designed to be able to carry large and heavy things for long distances. They have lots of stamina. They are the largest and oldest of the Arcitic sled dogs. They are named after a native Inuit tribe - Malamutes.*

- **Afghan Hound**: *The Afghan Hound originated in Afghanistan and the surrounding areas. They are sight hounds and keen hunters. They typically hunted rabbits and gazelles during ancient times. Afghan Hounds are now known for their long silky coats.*

- **Saluki:** *The Saluki is considered "the royal dog of Egypt". In ancient Egypt, their bodies were even sometimes mummified. That's just how highly the Egyptians thought of them. The Saluki is a sight hound and is very fast. They were strong hunters capable of taking down prey like gazelles.*

Other breeds:

- **Lhasa Apso:** *The Lhasa Apso comes from the Himalayan Mountains where it's very cold. Which is why they probably have such nice long coats adapting to their environment? They were guard dogs for Buddhist monasteries and in the homes of important Tibetan nobles.*

- **Pekingese:** *These dogs were considered more as pets than workers. The Pekingese have an interesting story behind them. Pekingese were allowed to be owned by royalty. If anyone tried to steal one of these royal dogs, the penalty was death!*

- **Samoyed**: *The Samoyed was used for a variety of different jobs during ancient times. The breed comes from Siberia where it was very cold causing them to adapt to their environment with the thick coat. The Samoyed breed was a reindeer herder, a hunter, sled puller, and a guard dog. These dogs were highly valued.*

- **Shih-Tzu:** *The word Shih-Tzu means lion in Chinese. This breed was another valued companion by the Chinese. They didn't appear to have any working duties. Today, they are one of the most popular pets in America!*

- **Tibetan Terrier:** *These dogs are characterized by having fur that falls over their eyes. The hair that covers their eyes is a means of protection from the cold climate and elements of Tibet, the country in which they originated. Tibetan Terriers are not considered true terriers. However, they were considered the "Holy Dogs of Tibet" because the lamas in monasteries raised them. They were mostly for companionship and believed to be good luck charms by the lamas, but they also did some herding and retrieving.*

Today's Dogs:

Through significant amounts of Crossbreeding of dogs over thousands of years, it has become extremely difficult to trace the ancient genetic roots of today's pets. There have been many new breeds bred and many mixtures of purebred animals to Heinz 57 varieties. We could list breeds forever, such as Collies, spaniels, retrievers, and so forth, however, all those breeds would be a book in itself. What is most important to know is what kind of breed you are looking for and its purpose. Therefore one should do there homework first.

However, the one thing we have learned is that dogs and humans have in common their intelligence and ability to not only be companions but to provide many work duties depending on the breed. We have learned that dogs have an innate ability to read a human's actions even if as slight as an eye movement.

Some breeds are loyal to only one person where others are family animals. Before purchasing a family dog, it is important to check out the bred and see if it meets your purpose. They range from quiet content animals to animals of high-energy needing workouts and daily exercise. Each breed has its own characteristics. They have developed their own importance in domestic society. Therefore it is important for humans to understand as much about them as possible.

When looking at a dog it is always wise to consult your veterinarian before making a final decision. It is important to remember the impact you as a human will have on that dog. We often say, "Dog is man's best friend," however, we should be considering "Humans are dog's best friend." Make sure before committing to a dog that you are ready to be committed to that relationship, time spent together and obedience training. Make sure you are choosing an animal that fits into your family dynamics and life style. Dogs are social animals and don't like to spend a lot of time alone. Once you have made a decision for your new family member.

Love it, care for it and remember to feed, water and take it to the veterinarian on a regular basis. The gratitude will be returned to you and in turn, you will receive more than you have asked for from this domesticated animal.

Enjoy your dog and remember dogs can pick up the same diseases people do so they need to be cared for and fed properly.

Listen to your Veterinarians advice on health issues so your animal doesn't suffer.

After all, you are investing yourself into another relationship. It is important to make it a good one.

Remember the importance of having your pet spayed or neutered so that it reduces the number of unwanted pets that end up in the animal shelters.

Also remember that there are wonderful dogs at the animal shelters including pure bred. Check there first when looking for a pet.

Once you have your pet make it a member of your family. This is a life long commitment and should be taken seriously.

Chapter 19 "Breeding Farms"

1. Puppy mills are nothing more than a commercial dog-breeding facility that focuses on increasing profit with little overhead cost. The health and welfare of the animals is not a consideration.

2. Puppy mills will breed female dogs every time they are in heat. For instance, a 5-year-old dog could have given birth to 10 litters of puppies.

3. Dogs in puppy mills, animals often spend most of their lives in cramped cages, with no room to play or exercise. They have little social interaction.

4. Often times, water and food provided for the puppies is contaminated, with bugs and whatever is in the environment. Puppies often are malnourished.

5. Puppies in mills are frequently found with bleeding or swollen paws, feet falling through the wire cages, severe tooth decay, ear infections, dehydration, and lesions on their eyes, often leading to blindness.

6. Almost all pet store animals come from puppy mills. At time of purchase, consumers are given incorrect lineage about the dog's health, breed, and breeder.

7. Every year pet stores across America sell 500,000 dogs, while 5 to 7 million dogs enter animal shelters.

8. Most puppy mills have no veterinary care, climate control, or protection for the animals from weather (hot, cold, rain, or snow).

9. Puppy mills have no cleanup control due to limited or any regulations or enforcement. This means that dogs can be living in urine and feces for indefinite periods.

10. Puppy mills are legal in most states. It is important that future pet owners seek rescue dogs from their local shelter or from a trusted breeder in order to put mills out of business.

11. Only 26 states in the U.S. have laws to regulate commercial kennels to prevent animal abuse and cruelty.

Sources:

Humane Society
Pet Adviser
Research

Chapter 20 "I am Dog Hear Me Bark!

I am cute and cuddly as man's best friend.
Don't get tired of me when I grow up.
After all, I have become part of the family.

Don't make me a part of your life until you can replace me.
I am forever loyal to you.
I have feelings for you now and need my family.

Don't make me your best friend until you have another.
I need love and stability the same as you do.
I get lonely when you are not near.

I'm not until you move.
I may not like change but I'll be happy wherever you go.
We belong together.

I'm not until you get too busy in your life,
Don't forget about me.
I have needs too and they include time with you.

I'm not until I grow old.
Let us grow old together.
I chose you as my best friend forever; I expect the same.

Love me unconditionally forgiving my faults.
It's very simple if you make room for me in your heart!
After all, you are in my heart.

Chapter 21 "A Dog's Prayer"

Dear Lord please send to me,
A human that will love unconditionally.

All I want in life is to be fed,
And to have a comfortable bed.

Some squeaky toys and balls to play with would be nice.
I need to exercise and walk everyday.

Should you send my best friend my way,
I'd be happy everyday.

I'd bark and snuggle to show content,
Hoping my best friend would know what I meant.

I'd love my best friend and be loyal each day,
I'd understand my human's needs in everyway.

Dear Lord if you blessed us together to grow old,
Our life would be better than the price of gold.

When the time comes for me to pass,
Make it easy for my friend to know it's okay.

So as I ask for my best friend you see,
I hope that you will kindly bless me.

Ruffff Ruffff (Amen)

Conclusion

Dogs are very social animals. They become part of the family. They have their duties whether a work dog or a pet. However, it is important that we remember to give them the dignity they deserve. We are responsible once we bring a dog into our home or family. It is our responsibility to see that they have adequate shelter, food and health care. It is our responsibility to interact with them and not forget them. It is our responsibility to give the obedience training to keep them safe. In exchange for what we do for them, they will be "Man's most loyal trusted friend."

Dogs have feelings and they never forget how they are treated. They know who loves them and who doesn't. It is important that one doesn't bring a dog into their home if they don't plan for a long-term relationship.

It is not fair to get tired of that cute little puppy and in a few months put it into a shelter where it may or may not get a new home. It is just as important not to abuse an animal, as it is a person.

It is important not to support Puppy Mills for the purpose of someone's pocket book. Take time when considering a new pet into your family dynamics. Do your homework and find out what would be the best for your situation. A good place to start is at the animal shelter. They can help you know which animals are better work animals, and which animals are better family animals, especially if there are young children in the home.

Most important is to love your animal and make it part of the family. This relationship will grow and last for a long time.

Animals require health checkups as much as humans do and make sure you are up to supporting the cost of a new family member.

Throughout the dogs, I have had in my life I have loved every one of them and enjoyed every moment with them. My biggest regret is that I am no longer capable of caring for a dog so even though I miss them I will not bring one into my home and not be able to exercise it, play with it, feed it, and enjoy the love and loyalty that I know I would get in return. I only hope I can help others to understand the importance of this.

To those of you that take care of your animals, I admire you. Keep up the good work and enjoy every minute you have with them. Remember this is a family member and a lifetime commitment. I will always regret having to give away several of my dogs due to living situations. It is an experience I never want to have to go through again.

Therefore, I will close with saying make sure your life is stable first. Animals require as much stability as humans do so try to be understanding.

"Dog is Man's Best Friend." Make sure your dog knows that. "Man should be Dog's Best Friend"

Made in the USA
Columbia, SC
24 October 2022

69475216R00075